Theology
of the Broken

Theology of the Broken

CATHERINE FAUROT

THE **BLACK SPRING**
PRESS GROUP

First published in 2023
An Eyewear Publishing imprint, The Black Spring Press Group
Maida Vale, London W9,
United Kingdom

Typeset with graphic design by Edwin Smet
Author photograph Sue Zeccola Photography

ISBN 978-1-915406-51-4

The author requested American spelling and usage for this edition.

BLACKSPRINGPRESSGROUP.COM

For Wil

Hands I have taken, face I have kissed, mortal I have ever touched,
it shall be you.

Whitman

CONTENTS

For nothing can be sole or whole
That has not been rent.

W.B. Yeats

UPON ARRIVAL

The names that seduced me have landed
on my porch, squat and unexpected
                                        as frogs:

pregnant Marilyn tulips,
silent Persian Fritillary,
Snake's Head, Aladdin's Carpet, Hokus Crocus —

demanding attention.

                    They threaten to bloom
too soon, to rot in festering conditions,
round shoulders clotting in the crate, fluted mouths
hungry for dirt, for darkness, for long spells
        of oblivion.

                    I dig for them
and they sing to me —

peasant songs from the smaller bulbs, tucked
like fingertips in the sod,
                            Gregorian chants
from the woodland flowers —
                        all of them bells that have not bloomed.

Each of these bulbs wants so badly
        to be something more.

We urge you to plant them as soon as possible.

HYACINTH

Penned in yellow netting, bag pursed shut
by the decisive metal crimp, these bulbs
deny their sulfurous itch —

                        and their beauty.

Cut free, they still cower in ordinariness.

But in the dark bed dug in the ill-kempt garden
they lie radiant, plump amethyst jewels spaced
across the loamy underbelly of dirt:

now a velvet lining, a casket,
a black basket for these purple-hipped seeds,
taffeta skins serene as they wait

for the shoveled clods of earth,

                    the God-awful winter

endured only for April's brief riot of scent,
their humped little run of pastel glory,
the Easter of childhood unpinned
from its crinkled, colored wrapping —

  and this memory
                of beauty planted.

THE MIXED BED

Desire is so hasty.

                The photo reminds me
to be cautious. Aren't those grape hyacinths? —
shrunken in their very name — although namelessly

compelling: minute periwinkle whorls,
closed like metallic jingle bells,
whirlpools of imperative smallness.

Also — are those tulips? Star cups of six
pointed flutes, bowls of light with gold fired
into the deeps, as if each one, in fact, held

dawn-grounds, or the rind of morning — but —
that orange-red — is it tawdry?
                               The lilies,
floating like birds, could be too much.

The whole bed: three by eight.
                            Really, I'm just
naming names. I know nothing about flowers,
    or how to make things grow.

                I'm so worried about spring.

THE DEEPER WELL

In the beginning of the story Joseph dreams,
but not of the well.
     No — Joseph dreams he's the fat sheaf.
He dreams he's the center of the universe.

But the well knows. She knows she's a pit, a hole,
a danger. She knows she's a cave and a cage.
     She is entirely receptive.

The famous coat pales in comparison.

Still, Joseph does not want to meet his fate.
When he falls he rails against the moon of sky above,
blue light mocking in its pure distance.

He weeps into hands that will work, that will serve
the pharaoh's every whim. His prized layer of fat
     burns off.

     The well suckles him, as she does
everyone who falls below the lines people draw
across their lives.

     Now —

          even above ground Joseph dreams
of falling, of the underground rivers that border
the land of the dead —

And the well dreams:

She dreams of desert rains bursting dry seeds into bloom,
dreams of improbable beauty,
        dreams into being gardens

        and the four rivers of paradise.

THE RIGHT EYES

(from Rilke's letter on Cézanne, Oct. 10, 1907)

for Conor

In the fall of 1907 Rilke sat
like Argos unflinching under Cézanne's paintings.
For a long time nothing, he wrote his wife,
and then suddenly

> *one has the right eyes.*

I was in a car explaining
the dangers of dusk to a son more precious
than breath.

In that air — I tried to say —
edges unbind, including yours. Day and night
stain each other
in the fading bluestone light.

He told me it's the best time to play.

Every night, this reminder: the pearl of the world
as it de-pearls.

Other loss constricts me —

but twilight's sadness is all possibility. The eyes themselves

— milky suspended fluid —

recognize their true home.

NARCISSUS

Who knew the garden-variety daffodil,
Wordsworth's strumpet flower strewn across all those fields,
flashing sunny undersides
                              in your mind's eye and mine —

and her slightly more modest sister, the jonquil —
        although that coquette will propagate
        just as readily if left untended —

all come from a singular flower —

                              Narcissus:

        named for the boy who refused
to fuck, who turned his face to his own face,
        solipsism of one.

*The bulbs we ship already have next year's flowers
        set inside them.*

                    I've chosen
my daffodils carefully. The Pistachio
has a pale-green tint, for the *chloe,*
the newness of spring.

                    I hope
they spread, multiply with golden abandon —
              but like the bulbs' namesake

        my own cold refusals have set — hard
                              inside me.

BONE OF MY BONES

(the rib speaks)

What a mockery.

The wound itself
— *when he took one of his ribs* —
even looks like a woman's miracle mouth,
red oval slit seeping blood in the very
first rib cage.

Words from earlier mouths
tell a truer story: man comes from woman
just as *ish* comes from *ishah* in the mother tongue,
not this backward, bastardized version.

It did hurt, of course —
cleaving along the center line, the heart,
through the mud-colored skin of the Adamah,
the earth-thing that we come from —

not the pasty, wax-museum man you think,
dainty male genitals dangling like fruit,
but Eden's hermaphroditic golem,
dazzling, androgynous angel of clay:

now split —

I

was taken out — what a loss — I
not you, *we* now a glued-together line,
juncture always the point of fracture —

even when we come together —
with the fumbling magnetism

of the cloven.

THE SEED ON BAD GROUND

It's not the seed's fault where she lands.

                            The sower
didn't notice the rock? or the blindingly hot
strip of asphalt across the yard? Not to mention
the daily proliferation of thorns.

The broadcast seed needs patience and cunning.

Let despair's harsh acid leech into rock,
breach the stones of the road,
                            patiently make dirt.

Inside the seed the sower waters the gardens of Isfahan.

                            Even
the lost seeds, scavenged by birds, are shat
out whole —

                or if they're broken:
                            are ground into light

                on the garden's fountains.

BLOOD ON THE LINTELS

In spring hope and death race each other.

Half the eggs in the incubator die.
Lambs are generally unlucky.

The ladybug's house is burning down.

If all it took was a little blood —
                    daubed on a door frame,
                            forehead, cheeks —
to ensure the passover of suffering —

                    dooryards would bloom oxide red.

We're slitting the lamb's throat now.

EVEN SOLOMON IN ALL HIS SPLENDOR

The lilies of the field, the sparrows...

I would like to be so industrious, bursting
orange in the sunshine.
                              I would like
to weave a nest with such ardor.

But on certain days —
                    blossoms decline all radiance.
        Petals close.

In the husks there is a shabby elegance,
louche suggestions of the sun's fecundity.

        I am done spinning.

WEEDS

Sown with the wheat, they flourish regardless.

Not, as the pious like to think, dotted
in the faces of others — but bound
              in my own hands, mouth, mind.

  I'm pious.

I tend my noetic garden. Some days
I think — those weeds are thin, tenuous —
until the spiny-leaved thistle flares
      cruciform,
                hot and defiant in the sun.

                  Or I think —
I'm John Donne in his later years, married,
all lust for courtiers' flirty verse mulched —
but lust for God springs from the same vast soil.

  The first sower sowed all the seeds.

BANISHMENT

Rumi's sunrise ruby lost all sense of borders
but the potted plant knows only its pot.

Its bound roots coil like tumors, its buds
stunt themselves, the leaves curl inward —

                                                resentful.

 I silk my own roots against curved clay.

In dirt, perhaps, the plant would be too frail —
or worse —

               could flower into something

                                     ordinary.

      The first curse is fear.

BROMELIAD

Who needs soil? Not this beauty — dangerous
as she is: pink spiked petals, armored leaves —
descendent of scrappy jungle plants duking it out
                          in the canopy.

She landed somewhere and she grew.

Of course all this is about a hypothetical
flower. I didn't buy the one that caught
my fancy — always, this nipping of dreams
                          in the bud —

but I've named that flower

                    — as I fall —

THE LOST GARDEN

Adam and Even left Eden, bickering —
the right half and the left half of the self
split, dirt from dirt.

                    My own garden was small,
an eight-by-three foot plot of potential, spring bulbs
packed together for maximum impact, a fireworks

display as short-lived as sex.

                    Really, on any given day,
how long can Adam and Eve cleave
together as one flesh?
                    Thankfully they have dirt

and work: digging, planting, the problem of thorns
and thistles a blessing in disguise, as is chaos,
the terrifying, fructifying summer growth

roiling up from the earth, life animated by the same
divine breath breathed into their uncloven body,
              the Adam/Eve.

                    Chaos took my small garden —
plowed with words, bed of hope — and I blamed
my other half for its loss, for the devilish bush
covering the detritus of spring —

                    the way Adam
blamed Eve
and Eve blamed the snake —

as if the hands that twine our beans onto the trellis,
that heave weighted tomatoes off the dirt
could rip living bulbs from their bed, would rip
                    words from the page.

He hacked down the offending bush, radiance dead.
                    Cloven, again.

In another garden Adam and Eve face the lackluster day.
They wait for the promise of dusk, for the night blooms
                    to open

and empty their scent into the memory of Eden
when Eve thrills to Adam's calloused fingers
and Adam digs deep

                    into their mixed, mixed ground.

DARKNESS COVERED THE FACE OF THE DEEP

His arm brushes my body
in the blank hours of the night —

and once again the first breath coils across the deep:
exhalation of space and time, the first

this not *that,* the two faces of God —

      spirit and the deep —

touch that raises the hairs
on the newborn skin of the first waters —

      breath like the mist

that later pearls the empty garden —

      O the terror of that kiss.

THE SECRET MARRIAGE

Violets are cleistogamous,
                              meaning
they partake in the secret marriage of the self
to the self,
              DNA that replicates

the plant regardless of bad soil, overgrazing —
conditions too harsh for the showy petals,
the pooled expectant nectar of the open flowers

pollinated by fame's truculent little bees.

                        Beneath the violet's
granny petals, beneath leaves functional as ears,
twined and curled pods hold all the necessary secrets,

                        the yin and yang
of darkness,

              the violent glut of blooms.

EXOTICA APRICOT

Getting the Most from Amaryllis

These bulbs embarrass me with their excess,
their unbridled ambition, their unapologetic emphasis
on beauty and the self.

Only their necks
are ugly: above the glorious chartreuse dermis,
the demure burlap skin is crowned by mottled closure,
muscular as beets,
brown as an anus.

Like all bodies the bulbs open.

I pay no attention.
In answer the bulbs issue stems topped by curved arrow buds
— pointing up! up! — thick and cock-like.
The relentless
cross-hatched cage they came in is still intact.

Only after I slit open the bag and bury
their flesh in garden urns
do I remember how I longed to bloom.

Now
three insistent green stems curve above lovely
dark soil, not yet watered but

— on paper at least —

home to flowers

made of dreams — *butterscotch with salmon netting* —

inscribed on voluptuous curls, tendril elements
proclaiming fecundity, abundance, the wanton

art of bounty.

Be patient.
Amaryllis can be slow to get going.

YOU WILL BE LIKE GODS

For God knows that when you eat of it your eyes will be opened,
and you will be like gods, knowing good and evil. – Genesis 3:5

In the dream a snake bites my heel —

                                        the moment
between not-bitten and fangs anchored into flesh
so slight —
                        the tendon a lyre string plucked
by violation.

                        Who said it would be easy?
The thrill poison of knowledge seeps up the leg —
or down the throat, the dusky chill of apple skin

against Eve's lips, the tongue's positioning flicker
against the forbidden orb, teeth their own violence.
Most times, about most things, we'd rather just not know.

But we know.

Render the grief of what is lost. The apple
sings inside your veins —*You are more, you are more* —
than everything that has been taken from you.

THE AMPUTATED LIMB

An open wound is a mouth with clandestine lust
for pain, the sharp eclipse of dullness —

again and again — any red thing but nothing.

It's the void that's dangerous.

               Any tree will tell you
that pruning is the wrong word —
                    even for a bald clean wound.

Ghost branches of the graceful limb rustle
while root ends, blind as moles, jostle for food.

Everything is hungry.

WATERS FROM THE WATERS

Let's pretend I'm just talking about my garden —

not the quicksand of life: the teenager's rabid
steps to manhood, my numberless litanies
of humiliation, love's loamy, spongy soil:

                                   I want order,
a Levitical tidiness, a sense
of exhalation between one thing and another.

The burning bush, after all, stood by itself.

 That radiance! — watered by the rivers
of Eden, steeped in wellsprings of chaos:

waters held back by the sheerest divide, seas
that still erode the earth's skin, my skin —

chaos that waters strange and brilliant growth.

Let me drink, let me drink.

THEOLOGY OF THE BROKEN

Life starts with rupture, whether
we begin the count at the birth sac's
split seams —

      or earlier,
        the moment the egg's skin succumbs
to the minute violence of a thousand thousand mouths —

    or the veil of the heavens tearing:

          the transition
from one world to another — *when the thing*
is no longer itself —

Next to the river I watch death inside
the song of summer. The water slowly
eats the rocks. A speckled trout rises

in the murk, spots like eggs
         across her predatory length.

In the garden — first the seed breaks.

           My own wound —

slit neatly like a tulip —

          pleats with joy.

FIG LEAVES

There is a kind of malicious shade —
                                        not
respite, not succor — but a shade stitched of fig leaves,
my nominee for the true source of evil.

Leave the poor snake alone.

                        Who hasn't gorged
on the forbidden, the lush crawl of *thou shalt not*
across the body's membranes.

                    We're hardwired to suck things in.

As for the ultimate source — who planted the trees?
Who made those seductive tongues? Who made the snake,
each crescent phalanx tucked into the exquisite next

of its newly legless body, while angels
juggled fiery swords in the world's first circus?

No — it's shame that makes the shade constricting,
shame that chafes Adam's nubile cock,
                                        that curtains
Eve's cleft with ominous darkness.

And fig trees grow! The one in my own life
is so hardy.
                It squats, omnivorous —

not over a breeding ground of transgressions —

                but over things left undone —
fermented batch of —

                nothing, nothing, nothing.

THE GARDEN AT MIDSUMMER

What if God is like me — a gardener
primarily concerned with potential?
                              I'm only good
at digging, with bulbs, the flagrant and delicate
possibility of seeds.

                    The bulbs bloomed.
It rained.
          The flowers — petals tissue-thin,
vibrant with sap — spent themselves in the way
of the world, beauty offered in flimsy cups
to the sun —
              and then scorched to pointed stalks.

                    I forgot
the stately stretch of July and August,
the meat of the growing season, forgot
to plant summer perennials, forgot my dream
of hollyhocks, St. John's Wort, the placeholder daisy.

What's left is relentless grass, tap-root weeds —

unless I wander out to the gardens now,
the abandoned beds —
                    to kneel, rip out, to plant —

dirt under my nails
                    like the farmer I married.

ORDINARY

for Galen

At the pond the girls harvest one glorious
fall leaf after another, stained glass mosaics
baptized at the water's edge.

                              My sturdy son
ferries his own wet offerings to the older girls,
constellations in his four-year-old sky,

                                        until
one scorns his leaves as 'ordinary.'

                 Nothing, I tell him, *is ordinary,*
          if you really look at it.

His leaf is the brown of steeped tannin,
pocked with holes, slippery with the afterbirth
of its watery gestation

                         into something else —

not Rilke's flame but the patience of water —

               lacework of space.

FRITILLARIA MELEAGRIS

Named for Meleager's sisters, who cried
so much the flowers grew tear stains:

the bells hang, blood-red in the shade,
freckled with rose spots — camouflage (like a fawn's)
    for apparent delicacy,
            like that of the sisters —

            Also called: Snake's Head —
a name manifest in the tensile menace
of the stem's deceptively innocent droop —

or Frog-Cup:
            conjuring an enameled chalice
for a humble amphibious queen, her forest of slender
  attendant leaves kowtowing gracefully.

       Less happily: Leper's Lily.

I plant mine in a border between sun and shade.

    Name me, I beg them. *Name me.*

FRITILLARIA PERSICA

There has been no success in the quest
for a truly black flower.
                            The best attempts
are conjurer's tricks, illusions of blackness

that vanish in light. Backlit by sun,
even that Goth beauty, the Persian Fritillary,
swoons with lambent attention, confesses maroon
flush, not lacquer but liquid capillary stain.

I bury their bulbs with trepidation —
                                    even the stems
are funereal, gray-green stalks like predatory insect legs.

I mix them among the gaudier bulbs,
but their specter haunts me like the dead ones
I've lost —

        tender black holes sometimes pierced by light.

THE BODY AS A LOOSELY IMAGINED ROSARY

The feet, of course, would be joined—
twisted into the drop chain above
the silver crucifix's anchorite.

Malachite beads next flare into legs,
open into the ropy candelabra of hips.
Here the loose freedom of the form
   allows for variation.

This morning I forcibly strung my self.

Within the pliable circle of beads —

     emptiness, the Infinite.

THE OPPOSITE OF REMEMBERING

Even before death we memorialize the dead.

That particular café becomes a dream of itself;
the garden's delicate zucchini blossoms
hang dry and papery under the glass seal of memory.
Boats sail with a fantastic crew.

Don't believe it was you alone, my dead beloveds.

      I left you too — caressing a shrine of the past —
smoother — smoother — than the last breath.

VIA NEGATIVA

Lucky enough to harvest my husband's
many-chambered hearts of garlic, meaty chard —
                    I'm counting curses.

                        It's commonplace
selfishness but I'll start with my own stringy
clematis, beetle-eaten hostas,
                    a large dead pine.

What I'm really cursing are the heavy sunflowers
of acclaim nodding along other people's fences —

                  but I never trained the vines, never even
shook out the fat, dry sunflower seeds into good dirt.

        Plant them with me now, beloved.

ON THE SAINTLINESS OF VAN GOGH'S CHAIR

from Rilke's letter Oct. 2, 1907 / Still Wed. Evening

The artist began as a preacher — or vice versa.
A brief stint at seminary, then straight
to telling the gospel to miners. Words failed.

Van Gogh began to draw

an old horse,
a completely used up old horse: and it is not pitiful
and not at all reproachful: it simply is…

In the Friends Meeting
I began to quake:

light painted me inside
and insisted on speaking —

but I said nothing.

…a chair, for instance,
nothing but a chair, of the most ordinary kind…

In the quenched-light of muteness everything starts to die —

but Van Gogh did not silence his brush.
He stripped off the varnish of silence
in a cruel process.

…how he renounced and renounced…in his paintings
poverty has become rich: a great splendor from within…

The chair itself
sang to him. He cut off his tongue
to taste it fully.

There it is: the gospel,

the light.

ROSE CUTTINGS

The rose canes twine fruitless toward the sky,
woody and blank, before erupting into razzle-dazzle
around the turned spindles of the porch.

The mossy, necessary silence serves its purpose —

                    but I'm tired

of the thick brown stalks, their unfriendly reminder
                    of lost suppleness.
Pruning is no fountain of youth.

I cut roses to start over.
                    Beginnings
always begin with a little death — in this case
internment in mason jar coffins —
        the intention being reincarnation —

        born-again roses in brown paper bags.

Months later I disinter fermented rose corpses,
translucent sprouts —

        The dead are still dead.

ANGEL TRUMPET

In the northeast it's potted and dragged inside
once the nights get cool, but the Angel Trumpet
            still conjures Babylon —

her priestesses who strolled in terraced gardens
at twilight, calling on Ishtar — suspended star
in the duskening night —
                    to whisper new hymns in their ears.

The flowers look like Gabriel's trumpet,
his angelic, extrinsic brass lily, trumpet that called
Mary, herself female & innately receptive —
                    to welcome the divine:

as they recall the lily between her legs,
fleshy and delicate as flowers,
striated salmon muscles —

            already tinged with decay.

DEAD OF SUMMER

Lilies and phlox — my neighbor said, abashed,
when I described my garden's premature
ejaculation — all spring, no summer —

in front of his own garden's staying power.

Phlox — as lumpy as the name — form mounds
of unassuming clusters, star-shaped but not stars,
          the aster's anonymous cousin —

ideal for filling in borders,
          famous for steady, old-fashioned blooms.

But I want a daylily that's not a true lily
but *hemerocallis* — from the Greek *kallos,* beauty
that blooms for a day, ephemeral —

                              I have
my eye on Pompeian Rose, its gold caldera
mounted by conch-pink petals, the color
                    of insides unfurled.

                    Each plant
produces an abundance of buds that flower through high summer
— almost into fall —
the gap in my life I'm looking to fill.

A bloom each day —
                    each day.

BEAUTY ENDURES

My friend wandered into death.

Before that winter I watered him
with Keats and Borges, wished him quiet breathing —

hopeless, while his lungs turned to stone —
not metaphor but name: *scleroderma* —
                    stone skin, sunk deep.

                    In my version

of the story the plant hanging on my porch —
a Wandering Jew — is named for everyone
who walks through the wilderness with eyes fixed
on the ten thousand soundless names of God.

                    This plant
is a star, a green-and-purple waterfall.
I need this jolt of hardy color,
the blood-sutra of the dying telling me —

                    live, live.

THE QUICK

That dream of an English cottage garden
was all larkspurs and cockleshells. I have

my own dead hollyhocks. They stand
unbridled in the sun, blood medallions
crinkled and receptive.

                  Once I planted
delphiniums that speared the sky — and my own
dismal gauze. The ghosts of pansies, of tenacious
Ozark Sundrops

      dare you to tell me I'm nothing.

CONCEALMENT

In bed in the morning I think
ah — to be a woman and have this man hold my breast —
as if I had slipped into this body, this life,
                    like a changeling.

What I don't say:
          my insides are radiant, a map —
          hallucinated sunbursts of joy, subterranean
correlations.

          Rilke wrote to Clara:
there is no need to share the tortuous and confusing
way to a work of art — you see, lover —

                    distance but truth.

I am painting myself from the inside out —
                    soon enough those colors will stain
                    me on the outside

                         — like an icon.

FIG TREE

On second look —

     the fig is the most erotic tree,
its glossy leaves pendulous and flat,
a repeated tricorn cock-and-balls motif —
  the fruit on top obscenely swollen and purple.

What a sense of humor those storytellers had —
or maybe an older, alchemical sense
of sympathetic magic
      or simply the rightness of things

as they are. For example, I'd like to be
a fig leaf plastered to a statue's marble organs
— such a friendly, nestling gesture —

or flagrant as the fig tree's sister, the pomegranate,

flaunting her unabashed blush-colored flowers
in Shakespeare's word garden, wanton apricot
petticoats unflustered by direct stares,

the late summer's globes of fruit insistent, thick-skinned worlds,
slick red wombs chock full of seeds, cavorting
with majesty in the wind, like their maternal

ancestors carved across the first temple's walls.

Both trees need hot, dry soil and water
at the roots — hardly shameful conditions.

I'm basking, basking
— my wounds in the sun.

THE GREAT DEEP

He split the hard rocks in the wilderness and gave them drink as from the great deep. — Psalm 78:16

Beautiful face, dressed in nullness:
motionless fathom before time —
                    no thing, no where:

Water me, deep.

I'm Moses, cracking the rock with his staff.
I'm the Israelites, crying for water —
water from the other side of the veil.

I'm tearing the caul that holds the waters
            from the waters —

                        with an empty jar —

MUD HOLES

I have produced a man with the help of the Lord. – Genesis 4:1

Women are blessed with one more than men:
holes the harsh thumbs of eons pressed
        into human clay —

the dusty, star-like opening
of the anus, the urethra's sleek one-way tube,
the carved Easter Island labyrinths of ears —

and like Eve all women conceive with divine
        aid.

As for the ripped opening of lips — that malleable
mouth is so voluble, so generally full of itself,
a traffic jam of words and food and sex —

we forget the site of the first kiss, God's mouth
cupped wetly, gently over the Adamah's nostrils —

moss forests, furred with life,
twin tunnels to grace —

                like any broken opening.

THE CATHERINE WHEEL

One wrist shackled to the wheel's rim:
    the future saint swings, terrible
        and unhinged,
crimped wrist cut by the pendulum's arc.

Alas, the kindness — the balance —
of next capturing the opposite ankle
    does not occur.

        Now both left hand
and foot are bound. She flaps
like a scab. She writes with a pen
    of gold paint not yet painted.

The wheel, which is time, rolls forward.

Inside the icon's crackled rectangle
    her other foot is bound by wires.
        Her life ebbs away.

This is what happens. She writes
the whole time. She writes on leaves,
on bark: on the dark road of childhood
    heady with the scent of dirt.

    Finally she clamps
the last free hand down with her own
golden thread.

        She rolls and rolls —
taut, ecstatic.

FALL

The catalogues drop glossy dreams like flowers
gone to seed.
                The dirt contracts into itself.

Gladiolas I'd forgotten burst their showy cups,
fronds falling like swords.

                    Things ready themselves.

Now the light slants through the trumpet vine's leaves,
green shards etched with veins,
                expectant as the crickets thrumming
hot and fast this Indian summer day.

                    The cup of the year topples.

A moth flying in the vine flutters:

    white life, white death —
                insubstantial as hope —

and the stained earth is ready for bulbs.

THE NEW ORDER

for Patrick

These bulbs are a gift to me — unexpected
flowering from a seed burst into its own bloom —

      and I scratch an extravagant future
onto paper: one hundred Pillow Talk tulips,
another hundred of the French Blend Rose,

a new moon's sliver of the silver-pink, seductive
      Angélique.

I know I'm dreaming. Who buys that many tulips?

          But in early spring
a small bare place by the back fence
will sport a carpet of fallen sky

      and somewhere feisty wildflowers
will dig in their roots for the long haul — Honky Tonk
and Red Crocus from Anatolia — whether

I move to a different pasture or return
      to till this same humble soil —

      the dirt of my life,
good enough to anoint my lips.

UNDER THE FLAMING SWORD

Evenings when Venus hangs on the horizon
like an invitation, Adam and Eve walk
      upstream toward Eden.

                        They watch
the angel's sword whirl through the dusk air,
fireworks swastika, white-hot, spitting
against the blue-banked embers of day.

The gate is the dividing line through everything.

Drifts of light from the sword float toward the ground
like sparkler dust, like sparks from heaven.
                            Eve's lips wake;
Adam's skin remembers it's porous.

Under Eden's spell of memory they couple.
At first Eve taunts the angel at the wall —
until the scent of honeysuckle from their bodies'
own gardens blots out guard and sword and gate —

                everything but breath.

ACKNOWLEDGEMENTS

The following poems have been previously published in these journals:

'Secret Marriage', 'Exotica Apricot', 'Fritillaria Persica', 'Concealment' (under the title 'Velatus'), 'Fritillaria Meleagris', 'Fig Leaves' and 'Fig Tree' in *Free State Review,* Summer 2018.

'The Right Eyes' in *Colorado Review,* Sept. 2012.

'Narcissus', 'Bone of My Bones' and 'The Catherine Wheel' in *The Westchester Review,* vol. 6, 2012.

'Theology of the Broken' in *Studio Journal,* May 2012.

'The Body as a Loosely Imagined Rosary' in *Bennington Review,* Jan. 2012.